WORSHIP:
The Missing Jewel in
The Evangelical Church

By A. W. TOZER

CHRISTIAN PUBLICATIONS, INC.
25 SOUTH TENTH STREET
HARRISBURG, PENNSYLVANIA 17101

FOREWORD

In 1961 when the late Dr. A. W. Tozer
spoke to the pastors of the Associated
Gospel Churches of Canada his messages
were recorded and he later edited them
for Advance, publication of the organiza-
tion. With the permission of the editor
these were presented in a series of three
messages on worship to the readers of
The Alliance Witness, and are offered
herewith.

WORSHIP:
The Missing Jewel in The Evangelical Church

By A. W. TOZER

IN the Psalms you hear a rapturous call to worship. They answer that famous question put to us by the Presbyterians: "What is the chief end of man?" The answer to that question is what I want to talk about now, and say to you that we were created, and after the Fall redeemed, that we might be worshipers of the Most High God.

God never acts without purpose; never. People act without purpose. I feel that a great deal of what we do in the church today is purposeless. But God never acts without a purpose. Intellect is an attribute of the deity. God has intellect and this means that God thinks; and so God never does anything without an intelligent purpose. Nothing in this world is without meaning.

God put the universe together with a purpose and there isn't a single useless thing anywhere; not any spare parts; everything fits into everything else. God made it like that. Science of course deals with the relation of things and their effect upon each other. But the plain people, the simple people, the people who

5

would rather believe than to know, and who would rather worship than to discover—they have a simpler and a more beautiful view of the world. They say that in the beginning God created the heavens and the earth, and that God made everything and put it in its place and gave it meaning and purpose and a task to fulfill in relation to all other things which He also made.

But God saw that the world wasn't complete, so as the poem has it, this great God who threw the stars into the sky and made the sun and holds all the universe in His hand, this great God stooped down by the riverbank and took a piece of clay and, like a mammy bending over her baby, He worked on this clay until it became a man and into it He blew the breath of life and it became a living soul. Amen! Amen! That's what we believe. We don't think about it in quite such a physical way as that, but we believe that God in His intelligence created the universe with intelligent purpose back of it.

And when we say this we know very well that some philosophies hold otherwise. But we pay no attention. We begin with gentle dogmatism. Now I use the word "dogmatism" because I want to be dogmatic about what I'm saying. But I use the word "gentle" because I don't want to become offensively dogmatic. I want to be gently dogmatic. I believe what I'm saying. I believe it completely. I believe it with sufficient emphasis that I control my life by it. It has been the reason I've lived and it's the reason, if the Lord tarry, I can die boldly.

Now, these plain people of whom I speak believe

that God created things for a purpose. He created the flowers, for instance, to be beautiful; He created birds to sing; He created the trees to bear fruit and the beasts to feed and clothe mankind. And in so saying, these people affirm what the Holy Scriptures and Moses and the prophets and the apostles and saints since the world began have all said. God made man for a purpose and that purpose is given by the catechism; the answer is, "To glorify God and to enjoy Him forever." God made us to be worshipers. That was the purpose of God in bringing us into the world.

I believe there is good sound reasoning back of all this. I believe that He created man out of no external necessity. I believe it was an internal necessity. God, being the God He was and is, and being infinitely perfect and infinitely beautiful and infinitely glorious and infinitely admirable and infinitely loving, out of His own inward necessity had to have some creature that was capable of admiring Him and loving Him and knowing Him. So God made man in His own image; in the image and likeness of God made He him; and He made him as near to being like Himself as it was possible for the creature to be like the Creator. The most godlike thing in the universe is the soul of man.

The reason God made man in His image was that he might appreciate God and admire and adore and worship; so that God might not be a picture, so to speak, hanging in a gallery with nobody looking at Him. He might not be a flower that no one could smell; He might not be a star that no one could see. God made somebody to smell that flower, the lily of the valley.

He wanted someone to see that glorious image. He wanted someone to see the star, so He made us and in making us He made us to worship Him.

I'm going to give you a definition of the word worship as I shall use it. You'll not find this definition anywhere because I made it myself. After Webster's done the best he can for you, then a good thinker ought to make his own definition. If you don't define, you won't be understood; if you define too much you won't be listened to, because there isn't anything so boring as a preacher who gets up and gives you a lecture on Webster; but if you don't define enough people won't know what you mean. You'll be talking about one thing and your audience will be hearing something else, and you may not mean the same thing at all.

I want to define worship, and here is where I want to be dogmatic. Worship means "to feel in the heart"; that's first—feel it in the heart. Now I happen to belong to that segment of the Church of Christ on earth that is not afraid of the word "feeling." We went through a long deep-freeze period at the turn of the century, when people talked about "naked faith." They wanted to hang us out there like a coonskin drying on the door. And so they said, "Now, don't believe in feeling, brother; we don't believe in feeling. The only man who went by feeling was led astray; that was Isaac when he felt Jacob's arms and thought it was Esau." But they forgot the woman who felt in her body that she was healed! Remember that? A person that merely goes through the form and doesn't feel anything is not worshiping.

8

Worship also means to "express in some appropriate manner" what you feel. Now, expressing in some appropriate manner doesn't mean that we always all express it in the same way all the time. And it doesn't mean that you will always express your worship in the same manner. But it does mean that it will be expressed in some manner.

And what will be expressed? "A humbling but delightful sense of admiring awe and astonished wonder." It is delightful to worship God, but it is also a humbling thing; and the man who has not been humbled in the presence of God will never be a worshiper of God at all. He may be a church member who keeps the rules and obeys the discipline, and who tithes and goes to conference, but he'll never be a worshiper unless he is deeply humbled. "A humbling but delightful sense of admiring awe." There's an awesomeness about God which is missing in our day altogether; there's little sense of admiring awe in the Church of Christ these days.

I like some of the things you do here in Canada very much. It probably started in a simple form and whoever did it first had a good idea—after the benediction you sit down and worship a minute. That's very good. I'm sure that for many it has become form. But when it's real it's a good thing. I see some occasionally who come in and bow their heads and worship before the service starts. Well, there's that admiration and awe. If there is no fear of God in our hearts, there can be no worship of God.

"Awesome wonder and overpowering love" in the

presence of that ancient Mystery, that unspeakable Majesty, which the philosophers call the Mysterium Tremendum, but which we call our Father which art in heaven. Now that's my definition of worship and that's what I'm going to mean from here on—that we are to feel something in our heart that we didn't have before we were converted; that we're going to express it in some way and it's going to be a humbling but a most enjoyable sense of admiring awe and astonished wonder and overpowering love in the Presence of that most ancient Mystery.

An awful thing has happened to us, brethren, when we can explain the Christian faith. I am just as much afraid of evangelical rationalism as I am of liberalism; they're both heading in the same direction. In the States now we have a new school of thought which goes by various names; new-evangelicalism, it's called, but it's neo-rationalism. The evangelical rationalism which tries to explain everything takes the mystery out of life and the mystery out of worship. When you have taken the mystery out you have taken God out, for while we may be able to understand Him in some measure, we can never fully understand God. There must always be that awe upon our spirits that says "Ah, Lord God, Thou knowest!" That stands silent and breathless or kneels in the presence of that awful Wonder, that Mystery, that unspeakable Majesty, before whom the prophets used to fall, and before whom Peter and John and the rest of them fell down as if dead, before whom Isaiah recoiled and cried, "I am a man of unclean lips."

Now we were made to worship, but the Scriptures tell us something else again. They tell us that man fell and kept not his first estate; that he forfeited the original glory of God and failed to fulfill the creative purpose, so that he is not worshiping now in the way that God meant him to worship. All else fulfills its design; flowers are still fragrant and lilies are still beautiful and the bees still search for nectar amongst the flowers; the birds still sing with their thousand-voice choir on a summer's day, and the sun and the moon and the stars all move on their rounds doing the will of God.

And from what we can learn from the Scriptures we believe that the seraphim and cherubim and powers and dominions are still fulfilling their design—worshiping God who created them and breathed into them the breath of life. Man alone sulks in his cave. Man alone, with all of his brilliant intelligence, with all of his amazing, indescribable and wonderful equipment, still sulks in his cave. He is either silent, or if he opens his mouth at all, it is to boast and threaten and curse; or it's nervous ill-considered laughter, or it's humor become big business, or it's songs without joy.

Man was made to worship God. God gave to man a harp and said, "Here above all the creatures that I have made and created I have given you the largest harp. I put more strings on your instrument and I have given you a wider range than I have given to any other creature. You can worship Me in a manner that no other creature can." And when he sinned man took that instrument and threw it down in the mud and there it

11

has lain for centuries, rusted, broken, unstrung; and man, instead of playing a harp like the angels and seeking to worship God in all of his activities, is ego-centered and turns in on himself and sulks and swears and laughs and sings, but it's all without joy and without worship.

Now, God Almighty sent His Son Jesus Christ into the world for a purpose, and what was the purpose? To hear the average evangelist nowadays you'd think that we might give up tobacco; that Christ came into the world that we might escape hell; that He sent His Son into the world that when at last we get old and tired we might have some place to go. Now all of these things are true. Jesus Christ does save us from bad habits and He does redeem us from hell and He does prepare us a place in heaven; but that is not the ultimate purpose of redemption.

The purpose of God in sending His Son to die and rise and live and be at the right hand of God the Father was that He might restore to us the missing jewel, the jewel of worship; that we might come back and learn to do again that which we were created to do in the first place—worship the Lord in the beauty of holiness, to spend our time in awesome wonder and adoration of God, feeling and expressing it, and letting it get into our labors and doing nothing except as an act of worship to Almighty God through His Son Jesus Christ. I say that the greatest tragedy in the world today is that God has made man in His image and made him to worship Him, made him to play the harp of worship before the face of God day and night, but he has failed God and dropped the harp. It lies voiceless at his feet.

Without worship we go about miserable; that's why we have all the troubles we have. You wonder why young people act like such idiots. Some young people have a lot of energy and don't know what to do with it, so they go out and act like idiots; and that's why gangsters and Communists and sinners of all kinds do what they do. They are endowed by God Almighty with brilliant intelligence and an amazing store of energy, and because they don't know what to do with it they do the wrong thing. That's why I'm not angry with people when I see them go off the deep end, because I know that they have fallen from their first estate along with Adam's brood and all of us together. They haven't been redeemed and so they have energy they don't know what to do with; they have capacity they don't know how to use. They have skills and don't know where to put them, and so they go wild and police have to arrest sixteen-year-olds and put them in jail. If they had been taught that they came into the world in the first place to worship God and to enjoy Him forever and that when they fell Jesus Christ came to redeem them, to make worshipers out of them, they could by the Holy Ghost and the washing of the blood be made into worshiping saints and things would be so different.

But not all young people have gone wild. I can show you young people by the scores and by the hundreds and running into the thousands who with all their exuberance have turned their eyes upon Jesus and looked full in His wonderful face; they have been redeemed and they know why they have been created. What Plato didn't know and Pythagoras didn't know and Aristotle didn't know and what Julian Huxley doesn't know—why they were created—these simple-hearted young people know. They know why they came into the world.

That's why I believe in the deeper life. I believe that the farther on with God we go, the farther up into Christ's heart we move, the more like Christ we'll become; and the more like Christ we become, the more like God we'll become; and the more we become like Him and the nearer we are to Him, the more perfect our worship will be.

I think that God has given me a little bit of a spirit of a crusader and I am crusading where I can that Christians of all denominations and shades of theological thought might be restored again to our original purpose. We're here to be worshipers first and workers only second. We take a convert and immediately make a worker out of him. God never meant it to be so. God meant that a convert should learn to be a worshiper, and after that he can learn to be a worker.

Jesus said, "Go ye into all the world, and preach the gospel." Peter wanted to go at once but Christ said, "Don't go yet. Wait until you are endued with power." Power for service? Yes, but that's only half of it; maybe that's only one-tenth of it. The other nine-tenths are that the Holy Ghost may restore to us again the spirit of worship. Out of enraptured, admiring, adoring, worshiping souls, then, God does His work. The work done by a worshiper will have eternity in it.

Acceptable Worship

GOD wants us to worship Him. He doesn't need us, for He couldn't be a self-sufficient God and need anything or anybody, but He wants us. When Adam sinned it was not he who cried "God, where art Thou?" It was God who cried "Adam, where art thou?"

Paul, in writing to the Thessalonians, referred to the time when Christ shall come to be glorified in the saints and admired by all them that believe He wants to be glorified. Those are a few proof texts in addition to the one I have read from the Psalms, but more convincing than any proof text is the full import and drift of the Scriptures. The whole substance of the Bible teaches that God wants us to worship Him.

Now, there are good, sound, theological and philosophical reasons for this. But while God wants us to worship Him we cannot worship Him just any way we will. The One who made us to worship Him has decreed how we shall worship Him. He accepts only the worship which He Himself has decreed.

I want to speak of some kinds of worship that God has ruled out. There's no use trying to be nice about it. The kingdom of God has suffered a great deal of harm from fighters—men who would rather fight than pray; but the kingdom of God has also been done great harm by men who would rather be nice than be right. I believe that God wants us to be right, though He wants us to be right lovingly.

The first false worship is Cain worship, which is worship without atonement. This kind of worship rests upon three basic errors. One is the error that assumes God to be different from what He is. He who seeks to worship a God he does not know comes without having first been cleansed by the coals from off the altar. But this kind of worship will not be accepted by God.

The second error is that man assumes he occupies a relation to God which he does not occupy. The man who worships without Christ and without the blood of the Lamb and without forgiveness and without cleansing is assuming too much. He is mistaking error for truth, and spiritual tragedy is the result.

The third error is that sin is made less serious than it is in fact. The psychologists and psychiatrists and sociologists and that gang of left-wingers that have come in over the past years have taken the terror out of sin. To worship God acceptably we must be freed from sin. Cain worship is worship out of an unregenerate heart.

And then there is Samaritan worship. It is heretical worship in the correct meaning of the word "heretical." Heresy is picking out what you want to believe and rejecting, or at least ignoring, the rest. This the Samaritans did. They worshiped Jehovah but they didn't worship in Jerusalem; they worshiped at Samaria. The history of the Samaritans shows that there were some Jews among them and that they had Jewish theology. But they had their Jewish theology all mixed up with pagan theology, and it was neither fish nor fowl but an unholy mixture of both. That is Samaritan worship, and our Lord said, "Ye worship ye know not what."

Then there is nature worship. That is the worship of the natural man, only on a very poetic and philosophical level. It is an appreciation for the poetry of religion. It's a high enjoyment of the contemplation of the sublime. When I was a young fellow and didn't know any better I studied, more or less for fun, the old-fashioned and now thoroughly repudiated doctrine of phrenology. It says that the shape of your head tells what you are. There are certain bumps on your head that reveal your personality. If you have a bump here just above your forehead, that's the bump of sublimity. You love the sublime.

Such are the poets; they like to look at trees and write sonnets. Well, there's a good deal of religion and supposed worship that is no higher than that. It's simply the enjoyment of nature. People may mistake the rapt feeling they have in the presence of trees and rivers for worship. Ralph Waldo Emerson said that he had at times—on a moonlit night walking across a meadow after a rain and smelling the freshness of the ground and seeing the broken clouds with the moon struggling through—he said he had often been glad to the point of fear. Yet Emerson was not a regenerated man. He did not claim to be.

I want to warn you against the religion that is no more than love, music and poetry. I happen to be somewhat of a fan of good music. I think Beethoven's nine symphonies constitute the greatest body of music ever composed by mortal man. Yet I realize I'm listening to music; I'm not worshiping God necessarily. There's a difference between beautiful sounds beautifully put together and worship. Worship is another matter.

Now, I'm very much concerned that we realize that the worship I'm talking about has a sharp theological definition, that there must be truth in it, that it must lie within the confines of eternal truth or it is rejected.

God is Spirit and they that worship Him must worship Him in Spirit and in truth. Only the Holy Spirit can enable a fallen man to worship God acceptably. As far as that's concerned, only the Holy Spirit can pray acceptably; only the Holy Spirit can do anything acceptably. My brethren, I don't know your position about the gifts of the Spirit, but I believe that all the gifts of the Spirit not only ought to be but have been present in His Church all down the centuries. The Spirit's gifts to the Church are the organs through which the Holy Spirit works, and He cannot work through His Church without the organs being present. You cannot account for Augustine and Chrysostom and Luther and Charnock and Wesley and Finney except they were men gifted by the Holy Ghost.

I believe that the Holy Spirit distributes His gifts severally as He will to the Church and that they are in the Church and have been in the Church all along. Otherwise the Church would have died the day that everybody who had been in the upper chamber died. The Church has been propagated by the Holy Spirit, so we can only worship in the Spirit, we can only pray in the Spirit, and we can only preach effectively in the Spirit, and what we do must be done by the power of the Spirit. I believe that the gifts are in the Body of Christ and they that worship God must worship Him in the Spirit.

But also we must worship Him in truth. Now the worshiper must submit to truth. I can't worship God acceptably unless I have accepted what God has said about five things. Before my worship is accepted I must accept what God has said about Himself. We must never edit God. We must never, never, apologize for God. No man has any right to get up in the pulpit and try to smooth over or amend anything that God has said about Himself. There is that passage about God hardening Pharaoh's heart. There have been books written to explain that away, but I will not explain it away. I will let it stand. If I don't understand it I will let it stand anyway. I believe what God says about Himself.

Then to worship correctly I must believe what God says about His Son. Not what some philosopher says about God's Son, or some theologian. I must believe what God says about His Son Jesus Christ our Lord. Then I must believe what God says about me. I must believe all the bad God says about me, and I also must believe all the good things He says He'll do for me. I must believe I'm as bad as God says I am and I must believe His grace is as great as He says it is.

Then I must believe whatever God says about sin. Here's another place where the psychologists and psychiatrists have done us great injury. They have euphonized sin. They call it a guilt complex. I believe that our trouble these days is that we've listened to the blandishments of these children of Adam and that we're afraid to see anybody get on his knees and get really scared.

Some of you have no doubt read of Peter Cartright, the great Methodist preacher who lived a century or so ago. Well, Peter was quite a preacher—an ignorant fellow, but God was on him. They tell how he once went to a conference and preached. The conference was in the charge of a little fellow from a seminary and of course Peter had little time for those boys. When Peter gave the invitation a lot of men came, including a big logger—a great big brawny fellow with monstrous, apelike arms, a huge fellow. He came down to the front and threw himself down and began to pray.

He'd been a sinner and he told God about it loudly, which scared this little seminary student half to death. He ran to him and said, "Compose yourself, brother, compose yourself." Peter Cartright pushed him aside, slapped the big logger on the back and said, "Pray on, brother, there's no composure in hell where you're going." Finally the man saw the goodness of God and the power of the cross, and the grace of God reached down and saved him. He leaped to his feet with a howl of delight and looked around for someone to hug and the first fellow he got hold of was the little seminary student. He picked him up and went dancing around at the top of his voice. It was hard on the young student's

20

dignity, but perfectly right nevertheless.

Now it is possible to have religious experience without Jesus Christ. It's not only possible to have religious experience, it's possible to have worship without Jesus Christ. That is, it is possible for a man to have an experience of talking with God or being talked to by God. Look at Cain. Cain had a religious experience, but God did not accept him. Look at Balaam, son of Beor. He had an experience and yet God was not pleased with him. In an old Catholic church in Mexico I saw a pale-faced old lady come and kneel down before a statue of the Virgin. With her hands together and her eyes open and her face set in worship she was having a real religious experience, but it was in the presence of the Virgin Mary. In a church in the United States I saw a huge statue of the Virgin, much larger than any person here; her bare feet were extended so the worshipers could kiss them and her great toe on one foot had been worn down with the lips of those who came to worship.

Yes, it's possible to worship but not be accepted by God Almighty. Brethren, I'm not sure but that those old pagans who believed in the gods of Olympia and Valhalla, who called God Thor or Zeus, were having some kind of an experience; but they died and perished nevertheless. It is not an experience that saves us; it is the blood of the Lord Jesus Christ. Worship is not simply having a solemn feeling about the length of time and the brief duration of our lives on earth and the vastness of the heavens and the smallness of our bodies. That may be beautiful but it's not worship. To worship acceptably, I repeat, is to be born anew by the Holy Ghost through faith in the Lord Jesus Christ and have the Holy Spirit of Christ teach us to worship and enable us to worship.

> "We praise Thee, O God, we acknowledge Thee to be the Lord.
> All the earth doth worship Thee, the Father everlasting.
> To Thee all angels cry aloud, the heavens and all the powers therein;
> To Thee Cherubim and Seraphim continually do cry,
> Holy, Holy, Holy, Lord God of Sabaoth:
> Heaven and earth are full of the majesty of Thy glory.
> The glorious company of the Apostles praise Thee.
> The goodly fellowship of the Prophets praise Thee.
> The noble army of Martyrs praise Thee.
> The holy Church throughout all the world doth acknowledge Thee,
> The Father of an infinite Majesty;
> Thine adorable, true and only Son;
> Also the Holy Ghost, the Comforter."

So says the old Te Deum.

WORSHIP:
The Normal Employment of Moral Beings

WHY did Christ come? Why was He conceived? Why was He born? Why was He crucified? Why did He rise again? Why is He now at the right hand of the Father.

The answer to all these questions is, "In order that He might make worshipers out of rebels; in order that He might restore us again to the place of worship we knew when we were first created."

Now because we were created to worship, worship is the normal employment of moral beings. It's the normal employment, not something stuck on or added, like listening to a concert or admiring flowers. It is something that is built into human nature. Every glimpse of heaven shows them worshiping; Ezekiel 1:1-5, the creatures out of the fire were worshiping God; Isaiah 6:1-6, we see the Lord high and lifted up and hear the creatures saying, "Holy, holy, holy, is the Lord of hosts"; Revelation 4:8-11, God opens heaven and we see them there worshiping God the Father; and in the fifth chapter, verses 6 to 14, we see them worshiping God the Son.

Worship is a moral imperative. In Luke 19:37-40 the whole multitude of disciples were worshiping the Lord as He came along and some rebuked them. The Lord said, "Don't rebuke them; if they didn't worship Me the stones would cry out."

Now, worship is the missing jewel in modern evangelicalism. We're organized; we work; we have our agendas. We have almost everything, but there's one thing that the churches, even the gospel churches, do not have: that is the ability to worship. We are not cultivating the art of worship. It's the one shining gem that is lost to the modern church, and I believe that we ought to search for this until we find it.

I think I ought to talk a little more about what worship is and what it would be like if it were in the church. Well, it's an attitude, a state of mind, a sustained act, subject to degrees of perfection and intensity. As soon as He sends the Spirit of His Son into our hearts we say "Abba" and we're worshiping. That's one thing. But it's quite another thing to be worshipers in the full New Testament sense of the word and up to our possibilities.

Now I say that worship is subject to degrees of perfection and intensity. There have been those who worshiped God to the place where they were in ecstasies of worship. I once saw a man kneel at an altar, taking Communion. Suddenly he broke into holy laughter. This man laughed until he wrapped his arms around himself as if he was afraid he would burst just out of sheer delight in the presence of Almighty God. A few times I have seen other people rapt in an ecstasy of worship where they were carried away with it, and I have also heard some simplehearted new converts saying "Abba Father." So worship is capable of running from the very simple to the most intense and sublime.

Now what are the factors that you will find present in worship? Let me give you a few of them as I go along. First there is boundless confidence. You cannot worship a Being you cannot trust. Confidence is necessary to respect, and respect is necessary to worship. Worship rises or falls in any church altogether depending upon the attitude we take toward God, whether we see God big or whether we see Him little. Most of us see God too small; our God is too little. David said, "O magnify the Lord with me," and "magnify" doesn't mean to make God big. You can't make God big. But you can see Him big.

Worship, I say, rises or falls with our concept of God; that is why I do not believe in these half-converted cowboys who call God the Man Upstairs. I do not think they worship at all because their concept of God is unworthy of God and unworthy of them. And if there is one terrible disease in the Church of Christ, it is that we do not see God as great as He is. We're too familiar with God.

Communion with God is one thing; familiarity with God is quite another thing. I don't even like (and this may hurt some of your feelings—but they'll heal) I don't even like to hear God called "You." "You" is a coloquial expression. I can call a man "you," but I ought to call God "Thou" and "Thee." Now I know these are old Elizabethan words, but I also know that there are some things too precious to cast lightly away and I think that when we talk to God we ought to use the pure, respectful pronouns.

Also I think we ought not to talk too much about Jesus just as Jesus. I think we ought to remember who He is. "He is thy Lord; and worship thou him."

And though He comes down to the lowest point of our need and makes Himself accessible to us as tenderly as a mother to her child, still don't forget that when John saw Him—that John who had lain on His bosom—when John saw Him he fell at His feet as dead.

I've heard all kinds of preachers. I've heard the ignorant boasters; I've heard the dull, dry ones; I've heard the eloquent ones; but the ones that have helped me most were the ones that were awestruck in the presence of the God about whom they spoke. They might have a sense of humor, they might be jovial; but when they talked about God another tone came into their voice altogether; this was something else, something wonderful. I believe we ought to have again the old Biblical concept of God which makes God awful and makes men lie face down and cry, "Holy, holy, holy, Lord God Almighty." That would do more for the church than everything or anything else.

Then there is admiration, that is, appreciation of the excellency of God. Man is better qualified to appreciate God than any other creature because he was made in His image and is the only creature who was. This admiration for God grows and grows until it fills the heart with wonder and delight. "In our astonished reverence we confess Thine uncreated loveliness," said the hymn writer. "In our astonished reverence." The God of the modern evangelical rarely astonishes anybody. He manages to stay pretty much within the constitution. Never breaks over our bylaws. He's a very well-behaved God and very denominational and very much one of us, and we ask Him to help us when we're in trouble and look to Him to watch over us when we're asleep. The God of the modern evangelical isn't a God I could have much respect for. But when the Holy Ghost shows us God as He is we admire Him to the point of wonder and delight.

Fascination is another element in true worship. To be filled with moral excitement. To be captivated and charmed and entranced. Excited, not with how big you're getting or how big the offering was. Not with how many people came out to church. But entranced with who God is, and struck with astonished wonder at the inconceivable elevation and magnitude and splendor of Almighty God.

I remember as a young Christian when I got my first awful, wonderful, entrancing vision of God. I was in West Virginia in the woods sitting on a log reading the Scriptures along with an old Irish evangelist by the name of Robert J. Cunningham, now long in heaven. I got up and wandered away to have prayer by myself. I had been reading one of the driest passages imaginable from the Scriptures where Israel came out of Egypt and God arranged them into a diamond-shaped camp. He put Levi in the middle and Reuben out in front and Benjamin behind. It was a diamond-shaped moving city with a flame of fire in the middle giving light. Suddenly it broke over me; God is a geometrician, He's an artist! When He laid out that city He laid it out skillfully, diamond-shaped with a plume in the middle, and it suddenly swept over me like a wave of the sea: how beautiful God is and how artistic and how poetic and how musical, and I worshiped God there under that tree all by myself. You know after that I began to love the old hymns and I have been a lover of the great hymns ever since.

Next is _adoration_, to love God with all the power within us. To love God with fear and wonder and yearning and awe. To yearn for God with great yearning, and to love Him to a point where it is both painful and delightful. At times this will lead us to breathless silence. I think that some of the greatest prayer is prayer where you don't say one single word or ask for anything. Now God does answer and He does give us what we ask for. That's plain; nobody can deny that unless he denies the Scriptures. But that's only one aspect of prayer, and it's not even the important aspect. Sometimes I go to God and say, "God, if Thou dost never answer another prayer while I live on this earth I will still worship Thee as long as I live and in the ages to come for what Thou hast done already." God's already put me so far in debt that if I were to live one million millenniums I couldn't pay Him for what He's done for me.

We go to God as we send a boy to a grocery store with a long written list, "God, give me this, give me this, and give me this," and our gracious God often does give us what we want. But I think God is disappointed because we make Him to be no more than a source of what we want. Even our Lord Jesus is presented too often much as "Someone who will meet your need." That's the throbbing heart of modern evangelism. You're in need and Jesus will meet your need. He's the Need-meeter. Well, He is that indeed; but, ah, He's infinitely more than that.

Now when the mental and emotional and spiritual factors that I've spoken to you about are present and, as I've admitted, in varying degrees of intensity, in song, in praise, in prayer and in mental prayer, you are worshiping. Do you know what mental prayer is? I mean by that, do you know what it is to pray continually? Old Brother Lawrence, who wrote <u>The Practice of the Presence of God</u>, said, "If I'm washing dishes I do it to the glory of God and if I pick up a straw from the ground I do it to the glory of God. I'm in communion with God all the time." He said, "The rules tell me that I have to take time off to go alone to pray, and I do, but such times do not differ any from my regular communion." He had learned the art of fellowship with God, continuous and unbroken.

I am afraid of the pastor that is another man when he enters the pulpit from what he was before. Reverend, you should never think a thought or do a deed or be caught in any situation that you couldn't carry into the pulpit with you without embarrassment. You should never have to be a different man or get a new voice and a new sense of solemnity when you enter the pulpit. You should be able to enter the pulpit with the same spirit and the same sense of reverence that you had just before when you were talking to someone about the common affairs of life. Moses came down from the mount to speak to the people. Woe be to the church when the pastor comes <u>up to</u> the pulpit or comes <u>into</u> the pulpit! He must come <u>down</u> to the pulpit always. Wesley, they said, habitually dwelt with God but came down at times to speak to the people. So should it be with all of us. Amen.